TERSE
VERSE

TERSE VERSE

A Collection of the World's
Shortest and Sharpest Poems

Cyril Fletcher

CENTURY PUBLISHING
LONDON

First published in Great Britain in 1982 by
Century Publishing Company, 76 Old Compton Street, London W1V 5PA

British Library Cataloguing in Publication Data

Fletcher, Cyril
  Terse verse: a collection of the world's
  shortest and sharpest poems.
  1. Humorous poetry, English
  I. Title
  821'.07'08   PR1195.H8

ISBN 0 7126 0011 6

Photoset by Rowland Phototypesetting Limited
Bury St Edmunds, Suffolk
Printed in Great Britain by
Redwood Burn Ltd
Trowbridge, Wiltshire

ACKNOWLEDGEMENTS

I am very grateful to Gyles Brandreth, G. S. Galbraith, G. L. Heminger, F. G. Kernan, Ira Levin, Leverett Lyon, Leonard Miall, Louis Phillips, Stephen Sondheim, Thomas Usk, Clifford Witting and Humbert Wolfe for kindly allowing me to reproduce examples of their terse verse in this volume.

I am also grateful to the following for their permission to include copyright material: Adele Aldridge for the three Not Poems originally published by the Magic Circle Press © Adele Aldridge 1973; Gerald Duckworth & Co. Ltd for 'The Hippopotamus' by Hilaire Belloc; the Estate of A. E. Housman, the Society of Authors, Jonathan Cape Ltd and Holt, Rinehart & Winston Inc. for 'The Elephant' by A. E. Housman; A. S. Barnes & Co. Inc. for the Geo-metric Verses by Gerald Lynton Kaufman © G. L. Kaufman 1948; the Estate of Ogden Nash, A. P. Watt Ltd and Curtis Brown Ltd for 'The Turtle' by Ogden Nash; Gerald Duckworth & Co. Ltd and the Viking Press Inc. for the poem by Dorothy Parker © Dorothy Parker 1944.

Where no author's name is given at the end of a poem that is because it is either one of my own efforts or else the work of that prolific, talented but exceptionally shy versifier: Anon.

Cyril Fletcher
Torquay, 1982

This is the tale of Cyril Fletch
of Terse Verse a discerning wretch,
He's made the odd selection here
And begs you to pin back your ear,
To start the day off with a larf,
Read a few when in the barf.

So when laughter gurgles down the pluggole,
You can then un-pin your luggole,
Happy that your merry mirth
Has given you your money's worth.

CONTENTS

INTRODUCTION

I first enjoyed Terse Verse when I was an Insurance office boy and read Beachcomber in the *Daily Express* in the train each morning. Glorious little gems brightened the foggy days as I tried to struggle into Show Business. (We called it 'The Theatre' in those days!)

> His Lordship from his Chair of gold
> Said 'All this marble's too damned cold,'
> So the Devil with a sly grimace
> Removed him to a warmer place!

and

> Alone on the lawn
> The Cabman dances,
> In the dew of the dawn
> He kicks and prances.
> His bowler hat
> On his bullet head.
> His feet are wet
> And his Aunt is dead.

I went in the evenings to the Guildhall School of Music and Drama and recited verse in the Elocution Class – being an incipient comedian I used to recite comic verses. W. S. Gilbert – hardly terse – was a favourite. But it was good to have a short sharp verse interspersed here and there to keep the audience and fellow students and sleepy professors awake! I won the School Elocution Prize. I am not telling this to you in a boastful way – it's just that in those days the poor soul who achieved this masterly stroke – this Gigantic Step on the Stairway of Fame – was asked to perform at Mansion House before the Lord Mayor and the Music Committee. They like to see some kind of return

9

for all the money that the City Fathers (Burghers) invest in the Arts. There were a pride of pianists, a virtuosi of violinists and a sonority of singers. I created a precedent by being funny. They'd never had a comic recitation before; I can see the heavy gold chains (and hear them too) in retrospect, heaving and gasping over the turtle soup contained therein, more like the ripple of the tide coming and going than the ripple of laughter.

It's fun to make a comic verse up in your head when taking the dog for a walk, or on a bus. (There is a hazard here because unknown to yourself you may begin to mouth them out loud.)

> Hear of Millicent Millicheap
> Who gnawed her knickers in her sleep,
> When she dozed off in a bus
> It caused a most unusual fuss.

In the first two series of *That's Life*, I used to recite an Odd Ode. The public still think I do even though I have not for the last five years!

> Cyril Fletcher in that chair
> On TV is calmly sitting,
> With the Public unaware
> He's sitting on Esther's knitting.

But a rhyme was sent to me recently to be read out as a misprint. It was a cutting from the *Walsall Observer*. One letter only was missing with this delicious result:

Arnold, Ernie passed away August 18th

> If Roses grow in Heaven Lord
> Pick a bunch with care
> Place them in my Uncle's ars
> To show that I still care.

The typesetter left out the 'm' you see. There is a thornless rose called Zephirine Drouhin. I do hope they used that, it has a long stem and is bright pink. If that happened at a funeral I went to I'd laugh so much it would not be necessary for me to go home.

I do hope as you read the gems in these pages you won't overdo it.

Wit needs the initial inspiration, and if it can have an elegance of phrase as well and be neatly rounded in a rhyming verse, then you can read it, or listen to it, with a warm glow of appreciation. There is a lot of warmth between these two covers. Some of it is well used but by no means worn. Gems do not wear out. It is good to have a new setting for them. Anyway I shall enjoy sharing this precious nonsense with you. A collection, one might say, through the ages.

Cyril Fletcher
Torquay, 1982

RUTHLESS RHYMES

Children adore the macabre. I like to think that the witches in 'Macbeth' rejoiced in the names of the Misses McDougall, McNab and McAbre and could be hired out for a small fee to liven up Hallowe'en parties and recite heartless verses like these . . .

Apprehensive Bertha Bright
Wore her garters much too tight,
Now she walks about on stumps
And comes downstairs in gruesome bumps.

Don't tell Papa his nose is red
As any rosebud or geranium;
Forbear to eye his hairless head
Or criticise his cootlike cranium;
'Tis years of sorrow and of care
Have made his head come through his hair.

I had written to Aunt Maud,
   Who was on a trip abroad,
When I heard she'd died of cramp—
   Just too late to save the stamp.

Making toast at the fireside
Nurse fell in the fire and died;
And, what makes it ten times worse,
All the toast was burned with Nurse.

Father heard his children scream,
So he threw them in the stream,
Saying, as he drowned the third,
'Children should be seen, not heard!'

O'er the rugged mountain's brow
Clara threw the twins she nursed,
And remarked, 'I wonder now
Which will reach the bottom first?'

Dear Father, look up,
Away from the cup,
And tell me what aileth Ma's forehead.
It's all black and blue;
O, what could she do
To cause a contusion so horrid?

'Your Mother, Jane Ann,
A newspaper man
Admired, till I warn'd her she'd catch it;
Like Washington, I
cannot tell a lie—
I did it with my little hatchet.'

R. H. Newell

Charlotte, having seen his body,
Borne before her on a shutter,
Like a well-conducted person
Went on cutting bread and butter.

W. M. Thackeray

'There's been an accident!' they said,
'Your husband's cut in half; he's dead!'
'Indeed!' said Mrs Brown, 'Well, if you please
Would send me the half that's got my keys.'

Mr Window Cleaner, you'll soon be well
After all, it wasn't far you fell.
You certainly received a nasty crack
Don't worry though, you'll get your ladder back.

Last night I slew my wife,
Stretched her on the parquet flooring;
I was loth to take her life,
But I *had* to stop her snoring.

Llewelyn Peter James Maguire,
Touched a live electric wire;
Back on his heels it sent him rocking—
His language (like the wire) was shocking.

An accident happened to my brother Jim
When somebody threw a tomato at him—
Tomatoes are juicy, and don't hurt the skin,
But this one was specially packed in a tin.

When I had my operation I displayed a lot of guts,
I could take it, smile, and like it, but the bedpan drove me
    nuts.

'Oh, Daddy dear, what is a basket?'
Said a youthful, mischievous elf;
'All baskets, me boy, are children of joy,
In fact you're a basket yourself!'

During dinner at the Ritz
Father kept on having fits.
And, which made my sorrow greater,
I was left to tip the waiter.

Father, I regret to state,
Cut his daughters up for bait.
We miss them when it's time to dine,
But father's fish taste simply fine.

'It is the same old game,' she said
'So play it how you like, my dear.'
'This time it's not the same,' he said,
Slitting her throat from ear to ear.

Little Willie, late one night,
Lit a stick of dynamite,
Don't you think he had a cheek?
It's been raining Willie for a week.

Little Willie in the best of sashes
Played with fire and was burnt to ashes!
Very soon the room got chilly,
But no one liked to poke poor Willie!

Willie in the cauldron fell;
See the grief on mother's brow!
Mother loved her darling well;
Darling's quite hard-boiled by now.

Little Willie from his mirror
Licked the mercury right off,
Thinking in his childish error,
It would cure the whooping cough.

At the funeral, his mother
Smartly said to Mrs Brown:
'Twas a chilly day for Willie
When the mercury went down!'

Willie, with a thirst for gore,
Nailed the baby to the door.
Mother said, with humour quaint,
'Willie, dear, don't spoil the paint.'

Little Willie;
Pair of skates;
Hole in the ice;
Golden Gates.

Little Emily was allowed to do
Exactly as she wanted to.

In an aeroplane she said one day
'In the cockpit may I play?'
Oh the switches and the knobs!
The gauges and the other jobs!
When she'd finished what a mess
And all because her mum said Yes.
She disappeared too in the prang,
And Emily became a bang.

THERE WAS A YOUNG LADY . . .

There was a young lady named Zanka
Who retired while the ship lay at anchor;
    but awoke in dismay
    When she heard the mate say:
'We must pull up the top sheet and spanker.'

A limerick, no doubt as you know, is the five-line nonsense verse that originated with the eighteenth-century alehouse chorus 'Will you come up to Limerick.' As a form of poetry it was made famous by Edward Lear.

Although at the limericks of Lear
We may be tempted to sneer;
    We should never forget
    That we owe him a debt
For his work as the first pioneer.

The trouble with Lear's limericks is that they tend to be remarkably respectable . . .

There was an old person from Twickenham
Who whipped his four horses to quicken 'em;
    When they stood on one leg
    He said faintly 'I beg
We may go back directly to Twickenham!'

. . . and the trouble with respectable limericks is that they tend to be short on laughs . . .

The Limerick packs laughs anatomical
In to space that's quite economical.
    But the good ones I've seen
    So seldom are clean
And the clean ones so seldom are comical.

In making my selection I've done my best to find limericks that are both decent and amusing. After all, in poetry – as in fancy dress – it's subtlety that counts . . .

There was a young woman from Aenos
Who went to a party as Venus.
   We told her how rude
   'Twas to go there quite nude,
So we got her a leaf from the green-h'us.

Here then are my favourites:

A girl who weighed many oz.
Used language I dare not pronoz.
   For a fellow unkind
   Pulled her chair out behind
Just to see (so he said) if she'd boz.

I wanted to offer you my choice of the world's best limericks, but given that 'Terse Verse' is designed for family reading, finding printable ones hasn't been easy.

The limerick form is complex
Its contents run chiefly to sex.
   It burgeons with virgeons
   And masculine urgeons
And swarms with erotic effects.

What's more:

The limerick is furtive and mean;
You must keep her in close quarantine,
   Or she sneaks to the slums
   And promptly becomes
Disorderly, drunk and obscene.

There was a young maid from Madras
Who had a magnificent ass.
   Not rounded and pink
   As you probably think—
It was grey, had long ears, and ate grass.

Said an envious erudite ermine:
'There's one thing I cannot determine;
   When a girl wears my coat
   She's a person of note;
When I wear it I'm only called vermin.'

There was a young girl known as Sue
Who carried a frog in each shoe.
   When asked to stop
   She replied with a hop
'I'm trying to get in Who's Zoo!'

There was a young woman named Bright
Whose speed was much faster than light.
   She set out one day,
   In a relative way,
And returned on the previous night.

Said a cat as he playfully threw
His wife down a well in Peru,
   'Relax, dearest Thora,
   Please don't be angora,
I was only artesian you.'

When accepting a young man at Kew,
A maiden said, 'Yes, I'll be true.
   But you must understand
   Since you've asked for my hand
The rest of me goes with it too!'

There was a young peasant named Gorse
Who fell madly in love with his horse.
   Said his wife: 'You rapscallion
   That horse is a stallion—
This constitutes grounds for divorce.'

When twins came, their father Dan Dunn
Gave 'Edward' as name to each son.
    When folks cried 'Absurd!'
    He replied 'Ain't you heard
That two Eds are better than one?'

There was an old man in a trunk,
Who inquired of his wife, 'Am I drunk?'
    She replied, with remorse,
    'Yes, darling, of course,'
And he answered, 'That's just as I thunk.'

There was an old lady from Ryde
Who ate some bad apples and died.
    The apples fermented
    Inside the lamented,
And made cider inside her inside.

The bottle of perfume that Willie sent
Was highly displeasing to Millicent.
   Her thanks were so cold,
   They quarrelled, I'm told,
Through that silly scent Willie sent Millicent.

There was a faith healer of Deal
Who said: 'Although pain isn't real,
   If I sit on a pin,
   And it punctures my skin,
I dislike what I fancy I feel.'

There was an old man of Vancouver
Whose wife got sucked into the hoover.
   He said, 'There's some doubt
   If she's more in than out
But whichever it is, I can't move her.'

There was a young man from Bengal
Who went to a fancy dress ball.
   He thought he would risk it
    And go as a biscuit,
But a dog ate him up in the hall.

There once was a monk in Siberia
Whose existence grew steadily drearier,
   Till he broke from his cell
   With one hell of a yell,
And eloped with the Mother Superior.

There was a young lady of Riga,
Who rode with a smile on a tiger;
   They returned from the ride
   With the lady inside
And the smile on the face of the tiger.

We thought him an absolute lamb,
But when he sat down in some jam
   On taking his seat
   At our Sunday School treat,
We all heard the Vicar say: 'Damn!'

Concerning the bees and the flowers
In the gardens, the fields, and the bowers,
   You will note at a glance
   That their ways of romance
Are totally different from ours.

A cheerful old bear at the Zoo
Could always find something to do.
    When it bored him, you know,
    To walk to and fro,
He reversed it, and walked from and to.

God's plan made a hopeful beginning,
But man spoiled his chances by sinning.
    We trust that God's Glory
    Will end up the story,
But at present the other side's winning!

ANIMAL MAGIC

Animals, being so much nicer than human beings, make ideal subjects for endearing terse verse . . .

THE RABBIT

The rabbit has a charming face;
But it's private life is a disgrace.

THE HORSE

I know two things about the Horse,
And one of them is rather coarse.

THE BUTTERFLY

And what's a butterfly? At best,
He's but a caterpillar, drest.
John Gay

THE OYSTER

Than an Oyster
There's nothing moister.

THE ELEPHANT

A tail behind, a trunk in front,
Complete the unusual elephant.
The tail in front, the trunk behind,
Is what you very seldom find.

A. E. Housman

THE FLEA

Great fleas have little fleas upon their back to bite 'em,
And little fleas have lesser fleas,
                    And so ad infinitum;
The great fleas themselves in turn have greater
                    fleas to go on,
While these again have greater still, and greater still,
                    and so on.

THE ROOSTER

Into the coop the rooster rolls an ostrich egg;
    The hens he faces.
'Not to chide or deride, but only to show
What's being done in other places.'

THE TURTLE

The turtle lives 'twixt plated decks
Which practically conceal its sex.
I think it clever of the turtle
In such a fix to be so fertile.

Ogden Nash

THE HIPPOPOTAMUS

I shoot the Hippopotamus
With bullets made of platinum.
Because if I use leaden ones
His hide is sure to flatten 'em.

Hilaire Belloc

THE MOOSE

Be kind to the moose.
He may be of use,
For hanging your hat
Or something like that . . .

THE AUK

The Great Auk's ghost rose on one leg,
Signed thrice and three times winkt,
And turned and poached a phantom egg,
And muttered, 'I'm extinct.'

Ralph Hodgson

THE DACHSHUND

There was a Dachshund, once so long,
He hadn't any notion
How long it took to notify
His tail of his emotion;
And so it happened, while his eyes
Were filled with woe and sadness,
His little tail went wagging on
Because of previous gladness.

THE PIG

It was early last December,
As near as I remember,
I was walking down the street in tipsy pride;
No one was I disturbing
As I lay down by the curbing
And a pig came up and lay down by my side.

As I lay there in the gutter
Thinking thoughts I shall not utter,
A lady passing by was heard to say:
'You can tell a man who boozes
By the company he chooses';
And the pig got up and slowly walked away.

THE CORMORANT

The common Cormorant or Shag
Lays eggs inside a paper bag.
The reason you will see no doubt,
It is to keep the lightening out.
But what these unobservant birds
Have never noticed is that herds
Of wandering bears may come with buns,
And steal the bags to hold the crumbs.

THE COW

The gum-chewing student,
The cud-chewing cow,
Are somewhat alike,
Yet different somehow.
Just what is the difference—
I think I know now—
It's the thoughtful look
On the face of the cow.

ZOO QUEST

'Stupid boy! Where are Elephants found?'
The pompous teacher bossed.
'They're never found!' the child replied,
'They're too big to get lost.'

SPRINGTIME

'Tis dog's delight to bark and bite
And little birds to sing,
And if you sit on a red hot brick,
It's a sign of an early spring!

MENAGERIE

The porcupine may have his quills,
    The elephant his trunk;
But when it comes to common scents,
    My money's on the skunk.

LIFE SPANS

The horse and mule live thirty years
And nothing know of wines and beers.
The goat and sheep at twenty die
And never taste of scotch or rye.
A cow drinks water by the ton
And at eighteen is mostly done.
The dog at fifteen cashes in
Without the aid of rum or gin.
The cat in milk and water soaks
And then in twelve short years it croaks.
The modest, sober, bone dry hen
Lays eggs for nogs, then dies at ten.
All animals are strictly dry:
They sinless live and swiftly die;
But sinful, ginful, rum-soaked men
Survive for three score years and ten.
And some of them, a very few,
Stay pickled till they're ninety-two.

NURSERY VERSE

Mary had a little lamb,
Its fleece was black as soot,
And into Mary's bread and jam,
His sooty foot he put.

Mary had a little lamb,
You've heard this tale before,
But did you know
She passed her plate
And had a little more?

Mary had a little lamb,
With which she used to sleep.
Too late she found it was a ram,
Now Mary has a little sheep.

Some folks say that fleas are black,
But I know that's not so,
'Cause Mary had a little lamb
With fleas as white as snow.

Mary had a parrot.
She killed it in a rage.
For every time her boyfriend came,
The darn thing told her age.

Mary had a little lamb
As dirty as a hog.
They asked her how it got that way.
She answered simply, 'Smog.'

Mary had a little lamb,
Cold custard and some prunes,
A pint of ale, a sip of gin,
And a plate of macaroons.
She also ate some apple tart,
And a little sturgeon's roe;
And when they carried Mary out,
Her face was white as snow.

Mary had a little lamb,
Her father shot it dead.
Now Mary takes her lamb to school
Between two hunks of bread.

Mary had a little lamb,
The midwife fainted.

Roses are red,
Violets are bluish,
If it weren't for Xmas,
We'd all be Jewish.

Little Jack Horner
Sat in a corner,
Eating a bowl of rice.
He sat looking glum,
And then stuck out his tongue,
And did something that's not very nice.

Little Jack Horner
Sat in a corner,
Watching the girls go by.
Along came a beauty
And he said, 'Hi, cutie!'
And that's how he got a black eye.

Little Miss Muffet
Sat on her tuffet,
Eating her Irish Stew.
Along came a spider
And sat down beside her,
So she ate him up too.

Little Miss Muffet decided to rough it
In a log cabin, old and medieval.
A bounder espied her and plied her
    with cider
And now she's the forest's prime evil.

Little Miss Muffet sat on a tuffet,
Eating her curds and whey.
Along came a spider who sat down beside
    her
And said, 'Whatcha got in the bowl,
    sweetheart?'

Little Bo-peep has lost her sheep
And looks for them sedately.
I hope that she will find them soon;
We've had no lamb chops lately.

Hickory, dickory dock,
The mice ran up the clock,
The clock struck one;
The others escaped with minor injuries.

Humpty Dumpty sat on a wall,
Humpty Dumpty had a great fall.
All the king's horses and all the king's men
Had scrambled eggs for breakfast again.

Girls when they went out to swim,
   Once dressed like Mother Hubbard,
Now they have a bolder whim:
   They dress more like her cupboard.

THE MONTHS

Snowy, Flowy, Blowy,
Showery, Flowery, Bowery,
Hoppy, Croppy, Droppy,
Breezy, Sneezy, Freezy.
George Ellis

LIFE'S PLEASURES

There are several reasons for drinking,
And one has just entered my head;
If a man cannot drink when he's living
How the hell can he drink when he's dead?

A round table, holding eight;
A hearty welcome and little state;
One dish set on a time,
As plain as you please, but always prime;
Beer for asking for—and in pewter;
Servants who don't require a tutor;
Talking guests and dumb-waiters;
Warm plates and hot potaters.

Little nips of whisky,
Little drops of gin,
Make a lady wonder
Where on earth she's bin.

A bumper of good liquor
Will end a contest quicker
Than Justice, Judge
Or Vicar.
                    R. B. Sheridan

A cocktail is a pleasant drink:
Mild and harmless – I don't think.

TOBACCO

Tobacco is a dirty weed. I like it.
It satisfies no normal need. I like it.
It makes you thin, it makes you lean,
It takes the hair right off your bean,
It's the worst darn stuff I've ever seen.
I like it.

Graham L. Heminger

"SMOKER'S KOFF"

IN PACKETS OF TWENTY

THE VIRTUES OF CONDENSED MILK

Condensed milk is the best in the land;
Here I sit with a can in my hand—
No tits to pull, no hay to pitch,
Just punch a hole in the son of a bitch.

CONTENTMENT

I'm glad the sky is painted blue:
And the earth is painted green;
And such a lot of nice fresh air
All sandwiched in between.

ELEVENSES

The 'Coffee Break' up in our tower,
Were better called the 'Coffee Hour'!
Leverett Lyon

VERSIFIED BIOGRAPHIES

CHAPS & MAPS

The Art of Biography
Is different from Geography,
Geography is about maps,
But biography is about chaps.

Some versified biographies are called Clerihews. Here are five by the man who invented this particular form of poetry, E. Clerihew Bentley:

'I quite realized,' said Columbus,
'That the earth was not a rhombus,
But I am a little annoyed
To find it an oblate spheroid.'

The digestion of Milton
Was unequal to Stilton.
He was only feeling so-so
When he wrote *Il Pensoroso*.

Geoffrey Chaucer
Took a bath (in a saucer)
In consequence of certain hints
Dropped by the Black Prince.

'Susaddah!' exclaimed Ibsen,
'By dose is turdig cribson!
I'd better dot kiss you.
A*tish*oo! A*tish*oo!'

What I like about Clive
Is that he is no longer alive.
There is a great deal to be said
For being dead.

Many of my more elderly readers will remember the BBC Chief Announcer, Stuart Hibberd – an austere man before the microphone and a merry man off-duty. He doodled the following Clerihew when waiting on one occasion to announce my wife Betty Astell and myself in one of our many radio series together . . .

The Odd Odes of Cyril Fletcher
Are never letcher-
Ous, otherwise Betty Astell
Would give him Hell.

Not all versified biographies are Clerihews. Far from it.

There once was a sculptor named Phidias
Whose manners in art were invidious:
   He carved Aphrodite
   Without any nightie,
Which startled the ultrafastidious.

Lizzie Borden took an axe
And gave her mother forty whacks;
When she saw what she had done
She gave her father forty-one!

There's a wonderful family called Stein,
There's Gert and there's Ep and there's Ein.
   Gert's poems are bunk,
   Ep's statues are junk,
And no one can understand Ein.

Clara Bow
(You may know)
Made a hit
By emphasizing It.
         Louis Phillips

Newton heard a sort of plonk—
An apple fell upon his conk;
Discovered gravitation law,
It shook old Isaac to the core.

John D. Rockefeller made a million,
Oh, hell, he made a billion,
When he turned up soil,
Voila! Oil!

Louis Phillips

Robert DeNiro
Is a screen hero.
Only a slob
Would call him Bob.

Louis Phillips

Tiddely Quiddely
Edward M. Kennedy
Quite unaccountably
Drove in a stream.
Pleas of amnesia
Incomprehensible
Possibly shattered
Political dream.

Leonard Miall

VISUAL VERSE

He went out one lovely night
   To call upon a miss,
And when he reached her residence
              this.
          like
        stairs
     up
    ran
   He
Her papa met him at the door,
   He didn't see the miss.
He'll not go there again though
   for

      He
     went
      down
       stairs
        like
        this.

HIGH FINANCE

He bought a little block of stock
   The day he went to town;
And in the nature of such things,

      That
      Stock
      Went
      Right
      Straight
      Down!

He sold a little block of stock:
   Now sorrow fills his cup,
For from the moment that he did,

      Up,
      Right
      Went
      Thing
      Blamed
      The

He bought a little block of stock,
   Expecting he would taste of bliss;
He can't let go and can't hold on,

The blamed thing wriggles round like this.

FASHION CONSCIOUS

miniskirtminiskirt
miniskirtminiskirtmi
niskirtminiskirtminisk
irtminiskirtminiskirtmin

legleglegleglegleglegleglegleg legleglegleglegleglegleglegleg

shoe shoe

MANIC-DEPRESSION

SOMETIMES I'M HAPPY
sometimes i'm sad
SoMeTiMeS i'M HsAaPdPY.

SUICIDE

And Now I'm here
From this here pier,
It is my fixed intent
To jump as Mr. Levi did
From
      off
         the
            monu-
                ment.

R. H. Barham

He rocked the boat,
Did Ezra Shrank.
These bubbles mark
        o
        o
        o
        o
        o
Where Ezra sank.

GEO-METRIC VERSES

CUBICOUPLETS

A CUBE HAS SIX FACES A CUBE HAS SIX PLANES
RECTANGULAR SPACES FOR METRIC REFRAINS
FOR COUPLETS LIKE THESE WITH A RHYTHM, OF COURSE
TO BE READ AS YOU PLEASE EITHER DOWN OR ACROSS
EVERY FACE IS A SQUARE EVERY EDGE IS A LINE
TO HELP YOU COMPARE TO UNITE AND COMBINE
TWO PLANES AT A TIME FROM BEHIND OR BETWEEN
IN THIS CUBICAL RHYME WITH THE VERSES UNSEEN

A CUBE HAS SIX PLANES A CUBE HAS SIX FACES
FOR METRIC REFRAINS RECTANGULAR SPACES
WITH A RHYTHM, OF COURSE FOR COUPLETS LIKE THESE
EITHER DOWN OR ACROSS TO BE READ AS YOU PLEASE
EVERY EDGE IS A LINE EVERY FACE IS A SQUARE
TO UNITE AND COMBINE TO HELP YOU COMPARE
FROM BEHIND OR BETWEEN TWO PLANES AT A TIME
WITH THE VERSES UNSEEN IN THIS CUBICAL RHYME

Gerald Lynton Kaufman

CHRONO-LOGIC

HERE IS VERSI-FORM DESIGNED
IN A SHAPE WHICH BRINGS
TO MIND, THAT WHEN PUT-
TING THOUGHTS IN
RHYME., YOU'RE
SUPPOSED TO
MEASURE

TIME

BUT THE
MEASURE OF
YOUR OWN, YOU
SHOULD GLADLY LEAVE
UNKNOWN; FOR THERE'S
SCARCELY ANY DOUBT, THAT
YOUR SAND IS RUNNING OUT.

Gerald Lynton Kaufman

AMOEBA-VERSE

Micro-picto-graphic rhymes
Enlarged 100,000,000 times

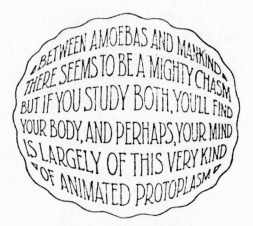

Between amoebas and mankind
There seems to be a mighty chasm
But if you study both, you'll find
Your body, and perhaps, your mind
Is largely of this very kind
Of animated protoplasm

Gerald Lynton Kaufman

NOT POEMS

Adele Aldridge

DOGS
DO
DO
DO

W O^m_a_n

Adele Aldridge

IMPOSSIBLE RHYMES

There are some words in the English language that defeat all but the most ingenious rhymesters. Month is one.

'You can't,' says Tom to lisping Bill,
    'Find any rhyme for *month*.'
'A great mistake,' was Bill's reply;
    'I'll find a rhyme at *onth*!'

Among our numerous English rhymes,
    They say there's none to month;
I tried and failed a hundred times,
    But succeeded the hundred and onth.

Christina Rossetti (who shed rhymes like confetti) almost managed it, with the aid of a well-placed apostrophe:

How many weeks in a month?
Four, as the swift moon runn'th.

Orange and lemon are as difficult as month:

> I gave my darling child a lemon,
> That lately grew its fragrant stem on;
> And next, to give her pleasure *more* range
> I offered her a juicy orange.

Porringer is more difficult still:

> The second James a daughter had,
>   Too fine to lick a porringer;
> He sought her out a noble lad,
>   And gave the Prince of Orange her.

Carpet and velocity were once considered unrhymeable – wrongly.
Here is a carpet rhyme:

> Sweet maid of the inn,
> 'Tis surely no sin
> To toast such a beautiful bar pet;
> Believe me, my dear,
> Your feet would appear
> At home on a nobleman's carpet.

And here is a velocity couplet from the dextrous pen of the clerical
poet best known for 'The Jackdaw of Rheims', Richard Barham:

Having once gained the summit, and managed to cross it, he
Rolls down the side with uncommon velocity.

Silver has always been regarded as unrhymeable. Stephen Sondheim rose to the challenge:

> To find a rhyme for silver
> Or any 'rhymeless' rhyme
> Requires only will, ver-
> bosity and time.

Ira Levin sent one better than Sondheim by finding rhymes for silver and penguin, another notoriously unrhymeable word:

> A woman asked me to rhyme a penguin.
> I said, 'Does the erstwhile Emperor Eng win?
> If not, I'll send a brand-new tractor,
> To 'Big Boy' Williams, cinemactor;
> On the card attached, a smiling penguin
> Will say, 'You're truly a man among men, Guinn.'
>
> 'All right,' she said, 'so now rhyme silver,'
> But I left because I'd had my filver.

A certified poet from Slough,
Whose methods of rhyming were rough,
   Retorted, 'I see
   That the letters agree
And if that's not sufficient I'm through.'

Of course, when you've got a cold you can get away with almost anything.

I sig the joys of soft ad suddy sprig;
   (I sig them through the dose).
      A welcob warb
We tedder to her spilig, verdal charb;
(She deeds the warpth), the robid's od the wig;
The blossobs their cobbigled scet exhale
      Upod the air, ad everythig here blows—
      The pik adebbodee, the pikker dose.

The Easter boddet id dorth-easter gale.
      The frogs are id the pod (ad id the throat),
The yug sprig labkid id the beadow sprigs,—
      Ah, warb, the all-wool labkid!
        Od the breeze
      A byriad gerbs of idfluedza float;
Ad by the stove, id witter fladdel thigs,
      I ped this soddet ere by figgers freeze!

When next you're lying awake with a dismal headache (and repose is taboo'd by anxiety) you could attempt to enduce a drowsy numbness by finding rhymes for Timbuctoo, Massachusetts and Niagara. It can be done – just:

If I were a cassawary
    On the plains of Timbuctoo,
I would eat a missionary,
    Cassock, band, and hymn-book too.

Of tennis I played one or two sets
On a court of Richmond, Massachusetts.

Take instead of rope, pistol, or dagger, a
Desperate dash down the Falls of Niagara.

Names frequently give poets headaches:

Chicago sounds rough
    to the maker of verse,
One comfort we have—
    Cincinnati sounds worse.
    Oliver Wendell Holmes

VAN GOGH, VAN GOGH, VAN GOGH

It seems rather rough
On Vincent Van Guff

When those in the know
Call him Vincent Van Go

For unless I'm way off
He was Vincent Van Gogh.

THE MODERN WORLD

CORRUPTION

Corruption's not of modern date;
It hathe been tried in every state.
John Gay

INCOME TAX

Something I shall never learn,
It fills me with grave doubt,
As to why it is called 'Return',
When I have to pay it out.

LOANS

Most banks will gladly grant a loan,
In fact they often speed it;
The only thing that they require
Is proof that you don't need it.
F. G. Kernan

CREDIT

Credit, like a looking glass,
Broken once, is gone, alas!

PAY

Whether you work by the piece or the day,
Decreasing the hours increases the pay.

BUYING AND SELLING

He who buys must need two eyes,
But one's enough to sell the stuff.

OLD LAW

The law doth punish man or woman
Who steals the goose from off the common,
But lets the greater felon loose
That steals the common from the goose.

That money talks,
I'll not deny,
I heard it once,
It said, 'Good-bye'.
Richard Armour

MODERN MEDICINE

The way some docs inject their flocks
Small wonder their patients fear 'em.
The cures produce burns and shocks;
They don't just prick, they serum.

THE DOCTOR

'Is there no hope?' the sick man said,
The silent doctor shook his head,
And took his leave with signs of sorrow,
Despairing of his fee tomorrow.
                                    John Gay

THE PURITAN

The Puritan through life's sweet garden goes
To pluck the thorn and cast away the rose.

THE EFFICIENCY EXPERT

Efficiency experts—
At least those I've known—
Can cope with my troubles
But not with their own.

THE BRITISH JOURNALIST

You cannot hope to bribe or twist
Thank God! The British Journalist.
But seeing what the man will do
Unbribed, there's no occasion to.
                                    Humbert Wolfe

COLUMNISTS

With all those expert columnists
I've carefully perused,
I wish I were as well-informed
As I am well-confused.
                                    Thomas Usk

COMMUNISTS

What is a communist? One who has yearnings
For equal division of unequal earnings.
Idler or bungler, or both, he is bound
To fork out his penny and collar your pound.

THE BRAVE NEW WORLD

With satellites and rockets hurled
About us willy-nilly,
The trouble with our Brave New World
Is that it scares us silly!

George Starbuck Galbraith

THE DOODLE-BUG

I was Hitler's secret weapon, I
Would doodle daily in the sky,
I travelled quickly wouldn't you
With fire and brimstone up your flue.

THE ANSWER

I know just how to cure the world
And make it safe and stable;
But I haven't the time to do it,
And those that have, aren't able.

Leverett Lyon

LOVE ALL

In Spring a young man's fancy
Lightly turns to love, they say.
And some, who otherwise are smart,
Get hooked for life that way!

Love is like a dizziness,
It winna let a poor body
Gang about his bizziness.
                              James Hog

A bachelor is a cagey guy
And he has loads of fun:
He sizes all the cuties up
And never Mrs one.

I remember—I remember well—
The first girl that I kissed.
She closed her eyes, I closed mine,
And then—worst luck—we missed!

'May I print a kiss on your lips?'
   he asked,
She nodded her sweet permission.
So they went to press,
And I rather guess,
They printed a large edition.

I recollect a nurse called Ann,
Who carried me about the grass,
And one fine day a fine young man
Came up, and kissed the pretty lass.
She did not make the least objection!
Thinks I 'Aha!
When I can talk I'll tell Mama,'
—And that's my earliest recollection.

Frederick Locker-Lampson

When I was young and full of life
I loved the local doctor's wife,
And ate an apple every day
To keep the doctor far away.

Thomas Lamont

'Twas in a restaurant they met,
Romeo and Juliet.
He had no cash to pay the debt,
So Romeo'd while Juliet.

Say it with flowers,
   Say it with eats,
Say it with kisses,
   Say it with sweets,
Say it with jewellery,
   Say it with drink,
But always be careful
   Not to say it with ink.

Women are like tricks by sleight of hand,
Which to admire, you do not need to understand.
William Congreve

Nelly's bathing suit
Is what you might call brief,
Just underneath her belly
Is a knotted handkerchief.

Love is like an onion
You taste it with delight
And when it's gone you wonder
What ever made you bite.

Here's a little proverb you surely ought to know;
Horses sweat and men perspire but ladies only glow.

She kissed him in the moonlight,
Her Mother heard the smack.
She said, 'It's naughty to do so,
So go and give it back!'

Love me lots,
Love me little,
Only leave me not I pray,
Much fatter in the middle.

A pair in a hammock
    Attempted to kiss,
And in less than a jiffy
They landed like this.

It is not fair to visit all
The blame on Eve for Adam's Fall;
The most Eve did was to display
Contributary neglige.

Oliver Hereford

When Eve upon the first of men
The apple pressed, with specious cant,
Oh! What a thousand pities then
That Adam was not adamant!

Thomas Hood

'Come, come,' said Tom's father, 'At your time of life,
There's no longer excuse for thus playing the rake—
It is time you should think, boy, of taking a wife.
'Why, so it is, father – whose wife shall I take?'

Thomas Moore

He used to call her Aphrodite
'Til one day he saw her in her nightie,
Minus teeth, and hair all frizz—
Today he simply calls her Liz.

The knot was tied; the pair were
    wed,
And then the smiling bridegroom
    said
Unto the preacher, 'Shall I pay
To you the usual fee today,
Or would you have me wait a year
And give you then a hundred clear,
If I should find the married state
As happy as I estimate?'
The preacher lost no time in
    thought,
To his reply no study brought,
There were no wrinkles on his
    brow;
He said 'I'll take the money now.'

I have come to the conclusion
Having given it a test,
That of all my wife's relations,
I like myself the best.

'Tis easy enough to be twenty-one:
'Tis easy enough to marry;
But when you try both games at once,
'Tis a bloody big load to carry.

The glances over cocktails,
That seemed to be so sweet,
Don't seem quite so amorous
Over the shredded wheat.

By the time you swear you're his,
    Shivering and sighing,
And he vows his passion is
    Infinite, undying—
Lady make a note of this:
    One of you is lying.

Dorothy Parker

THAT'S LIFE

I wonder who wrote this . . .?

In *That's Life* Esther Rantzen would stretch
For hours the defaults of some wretch,
    Whilst the wittiest bits
    (Which had us in fits)
Came from that chap in the chair Cyril Fletch!

Don't worry if your life's a joke,
And your successes few;
Remember that the mighty oak
Was once a nut like you!

I have never had a piece of toast
Particularly long and wide,
But fell upon the sanded floor,
And always on the buttered side.
                    James Payne

Don't tell your friends about your Indigestion:
'How are you!' is a Greeting, not a Question.
Arthur Guiterman

God and the Doctor we alike adore,
But only when in danger, not before;
The danger o'er, both are alike requited,
God is forgotten, and the doctor slighted.
John Owen

CHEATING

Doubtless the pleasure is as great
Of being cheated, as to cheat.
As lookers-on feel most delight,
That least perceive a juggler's sleight,
And still the less they understand,
The more th'admire his sleight of hand.
Samuel Butler

The rain it raineth on the just,
And also on the unjust fella;
But chiefly on the just, because,
The unjust steals the just's umbrella.
                                    G. F. Bowen

I never forget a favour
Although I must admit it
Does seem to have more flavour
When I'm the one who did it!
S. Omar Barker

Hatred is by far the longest pleasure;
Men love in haste – but they detest at leisure.
Lord Byron

Those who in quarrels interpose
Must often wipe a bloody nose.
John Gay

People who live in Chateaux
Should never throw tomateaux.

The Christian is a man who feels
Repentance on a Sunday
For what he did on Saturday
And is going to do on Monday.
                              T. R. Ybarra

If all good people were clever,
    And all clever people were good,
The world would be nicer than ever,
    We thought it possibly could.
But somehow, 'tis seldom or never
    The two hit it off as they should;
The good are so harsh to the clever,
    The clever so rude to the good!
                              Elizabeth Wordsworth

'Thrice is he armed
That hath his quarrel just.'
And four times he
Who gets his fist in fust.
Artemus Ward

THE PESSIMIST

Nothing to do but work,
Nothing to eat but food,
Nothing to wear but clothes
To keep one from going nude.
Benjamin King

Twixt the optimist and pessimist
The difference is droll;
The optimist sees the doughnut,
The pessimist sees, the hole.

McLandburgh Wilson

'Tis easy enough to be pleasant,
When life flows by with a whistle,
   But the man worthwhile
   Is the man with a smile,
When he sits down on a thistle.

If, of all words of tongue and pen,
The saddest are, 'IT MIGHT HAVE BEEN,'
More sad are these we daily see:
'IT IS, BUT HADN'T OUGHT TO BE!'
Bret Harte

See the happy Moron,
He doesn't give a damn.
I wish I was a moron—
My God, perhaps I am.

I'd rather be handsome than homely;
I'd rather be youthful than old;
If I can't have a bushel of silver,
I'll do with a barrel of gold.
James Geoffrey Roche

It is remarkable that they
Talk most who have the least to say.
Matthew Prior

'Tis an old maxim in the schools,
That flattery's the food of fools;
Yet now and then your men of wit
Will condescend to take a bit.
Jonathan Swift

O wad some power the giftie gie us
To see some people before they see us.
Ethel Watts Mumford

Society is now one polished horde,
Formed by two mighty tribes – the bores and bored.
Lord Byron

Inspiration and genius
Are not everything.
While Dickens wrote
The telephone didn't ring.

Now you who rhyme, and I who rhyme,
Have not we sworn it, many a time,
That we no more our verse would scrawl,
For Shakespeare he had said it all!
Richard Watson Gilder

THAT'S DEATH

In Los Angeles known as LA
Talk of dying was never OK
So their dead little baskets
Were enveloped in caskets
And the funeral became a ballet.*

This is the grave of Mike O'Day,
Who died maintaining his right of way,
His right was clear, his will was strong,
But he's just as dead as if he'd been wrong.

Here lie I and my four daughters,
Killed by drinking Cheltenham waters,
Had we but stuck to Epsom salts,
We wouldn't have been in these here vaults.

*American pronunciation please.

Here lies the body of Mary Ann Lowder,
She burst while drinking a Seidlitz powder.
Called from the world to her Heavenly rest,
She should have waited 'til it effervesced.

Here Einstein lies;
    At least they laid his bier
Just hereabouts—
    Or relatively near.

Here lies old thirty-three-and-a-third per cent
The more he got the more he lent,
The more he lent the more he craved—
Good Lord, can such a man be saved?

The bomb he set went off too soon,
And here his story ceases.
The bits they found are buried here—
So thus he Rests in Pieces.

Old Tom is gone (too soon alas!)
He tried to trace escaping gas.
With lighted match he braved the fates
Which blew him to the Pearly Gates.

Here lies a man who met his fate
Because he put on too much weight.
To over-eating he was prone
But now he's gained his final STONE.

Here rests the body of our MP
Who promised lots for you and me.
His words his deeds did not fulfil
And though he's dead he's LYING STILL.

In crossing o'er the fatal bridge
John Morris he was slain.
But it was not by mortal hand
But by a railway train.

My wife is dead, and here she lies
Nobody laughs, and nobody cries;
Where she has gone, or how she fares
Nobody knows, and nobody cares.

Here lies Squire Berry,
Who never would marry,
Nor ever gave ought to the poor.
He lived like a hog,
And died like a dog,
And left all he had to a Wh**e.

Here lies the body of Martha Dias
Who was always uneasy, and not overpious;
She lived to the age of three score and ten,
And gave to the worms what she refused to men.

Beneath this silent stone is laid
A noisy antiquated maid,
Who from her cradle talked till death,
And ne'er before was out of breath.

Here lies my wife:
Here let her lie!
Now she's at rest,
And so am I.
        John Dryden

Here lies a woman, no man can deny it,
She died in peace, although she lived unquiet;
Here husband prays, if e'er this way you walk,
You would tread softly – If she wake she'll talk.

Here lies a chump who got no gain
From jumping on a moving train.
Banana skins on platform seven
Ensured his terminus was Heaven.

Here lies the mother of children seven,
Four on earth and three in Heaven;
The three in Heaven preferring rather
To die with mother than live with father.

He passed the bobby without any fuss,
And he passed a cart of hay,
He tried to pass a swerving bus,
And then he passed away.

Here lies John Bunn,
He was killed by a gun.
His name was not Bunn, but Wood,
But Wood would not rhyme with Gun
    And Bunn would.

Here lies the body of our Anna
Done to death by a banana.
It wasn't the fruit that laid her low
But the skin of the thing that made
    her go.

This spot is the sweetest I've seen in my life,
For it raises my flowers, and covers my wife.

Life is a jest, and all things show it,
I thought so once, but now I know it.
                                                    John Gay

'I miss my husband so!'
    The woman cried.
And so just one more shot
    At him she tried.

Finally, the shortest poem in the history of English Literature:

ODE TO A GOLDFISH

O
Wet
Pet!

Gyles Brandreth